Soccer

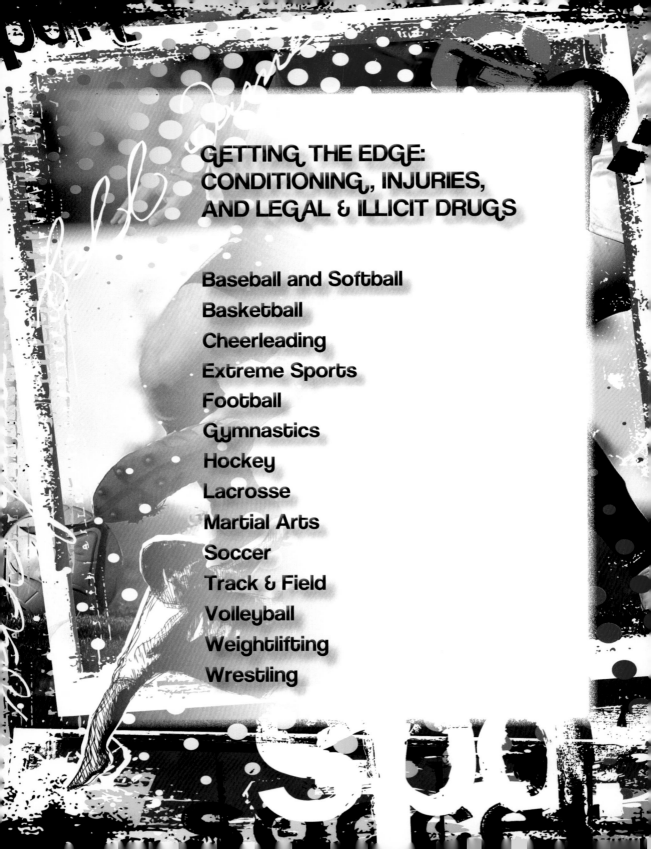

GETTING THE EDGE: CONDITIONING, INJURIES, AND LEGAL & ILLICIT DRUGS

Soccer

by J. S. McIntosh

MC PUBLISHERS

Mason Crest Publishers

MASON CREST PUBLISHERS INC.
370 Reed Road
Broomall, Pennsylvania 19008
(866)MCP-BOOK (toll free)
www.masoncrest.com

First Printing
9 8 7 6 5 4 3 2 1

Library of Congress Cataloging-in-Publication Data

McIntosh, J. S.
  Soccer / by J. S. McIntosh.
    p. cm. — (Getting the edge : conditioning, injuries, and legal & illicit drugs)
  Includes bibliographical references and index.
  ISBN 978-1-4222-1739-9   ISBN (series) 978-1-4222-1728-3
  1. Soccer—Juvenile literature. 2. Soccer—Training—Juvenile literature. I.
Title.
  GV943.25.M36 2011
  796.334—dc22
                                    2010015259

Produced by Harding House Publishing Service, Inc.
www.hardinghousepages.com
Interior Design by MK Bassett-Harvey.
Cover Design by Torque Advertising + Design.
Printed in the USA by Bang Printing.

The creators of this book have made every effort to provide accurate information, but it should not be used as a substitute for the help and services of trained professionals.

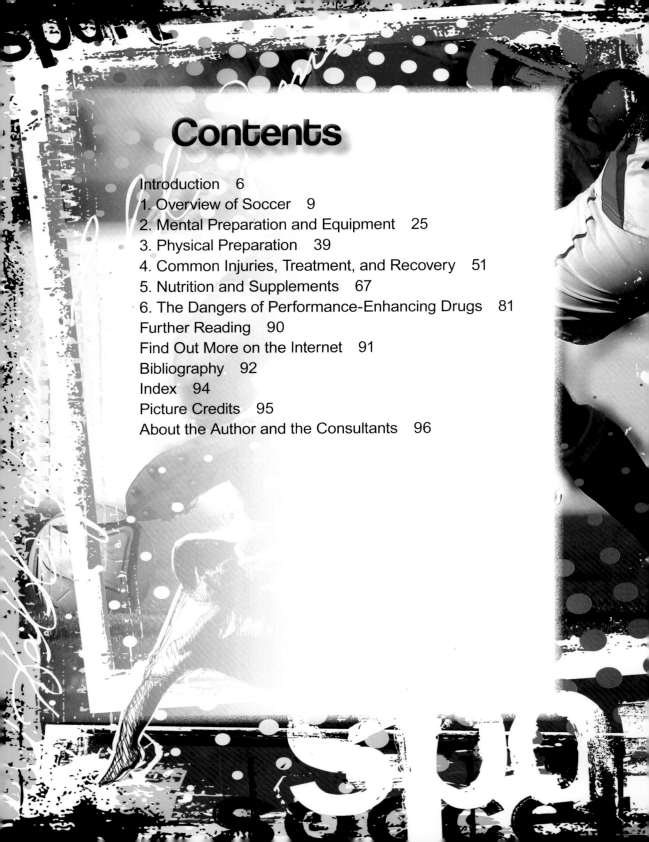

Contents

Introduction

GETTING THE EDGE: CONDITIONING, INJURIES, AND LEGAL & ILLICIT DRUGS is a four-teen-volume series written for young people who are interested in learning about various sports and how to participate in them safely. Each volume examines the history of the sport and the rules of play; it also acts as a guide for prevention and treatment of injuries, and includes instruction on stretching, warming up, and strength training, all of which can help play-ers avoid the most common musculoskeletal injuries. Each volume also includes tips on healthy nutrition for athletes, as well as information on the risks of using performance-enhancing drugs or other illegal substances. GETTING THE EDGE offers ways for readers to healthily and legally improve their performance and gain more enjoyment from playing sports. Young athletes will find these volumes informative and helpful in their pursuit of excellence.

Sports medicine professionals assigned to a sport with which they are not familiar can also benefit from this series. For example, a football ath-letic trainer may need to provide medical care for a local gymnastics meet. Although the emergency medical principles and action plan would remain the same, the athletic trainer could provide better care for the gymnasts after reading a simple overview of the principles of gymnastics in GETTING THE EDGE.

Although these books offer an overview, they are not intended to be comprehensive in the recognition and management of sports injuries. They should not replace the professional advice of a trainer, doctor, or nutrition-ist. The text helps the reader appreciate and gain awareness of the sport's history, standard training techniques, common injuries, dietary guidelines,

goal

and the dangers of using drugs to gain an advantage. Reference material and directed readings are provided for those who want to delve further into these subjects.

Written in a direct and easily accessible style, GETTING THE EDGE is an enjoyable series that will help young people learn about sports and sports medicine.

—*Susan Saliba, Ph.D., National Athletic Trainers' Association Education Council*

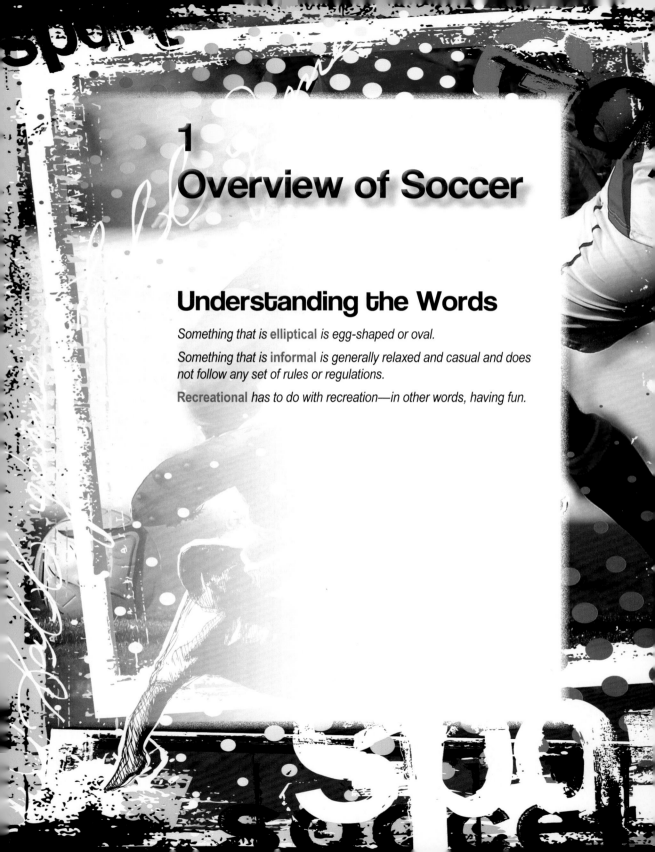

1
Overview of Soccer

Understanding the Words

*Something that is **elliptical** is egg-shaped or oval.*

*Something that is **informal** is generally relaxed and casual and does not follow any set of rules or regulations.*

***Recreational** has to do with recreation—in other words, having fun.*

goal

Soccer, football, fútbol, koura el-khadim, "the beautiful game," footy—whatever you call it, it is considered by many people to be the most popular sport in the world. Billions of people play or watch soccer worldwide, and the international football association, FIFA, has an annual income of over $700 million.

DID YOU KNOW?

In the nineteenth century, goal posts were narrower and taller. The referee was only a timekeeper who stayed on the sidelines.

The Cambridge rules for soccer were first recorded in 1848. No rules were universally adopted until 1863 when the Cambridge rules were revised by a committee.

SOCCER

goal

History

Ancient forms of soccer go back five thousand years. Archeologists have found evidence of sports played with balls in several continents. When the Pilgrims landed on the shores of Massachusetts, they found Native Americans playing a soccer-like game called pasuckuakohowog, which means, "they gather to play ball with the foot." The Greeks used inflated ox bladders, the Egyptians played with straw balls, and the Aztecs used rubber. Charles Goodyear, an American from Connecticut, invented the modern soccer ball, inflated rubber covered in leather.

> ### DID YOU KNOW?
> In 1871, the first international soccer match took place when Scotland traveled south to face England.

Modern soccer began in private universities of England in the nineteenth century. For a while, there was no set of rules that were agreed upon and practiced, but in 1863, team representatives met in a London tavern and agreed to play by the Cambridge University rules that had been drawn up seventeen years earlier. This became the first football association.

In the late 1800s, Britain was the world's major trading nation, and its soldiers, sailors, merchants, and engineers spread soccer across the globe. Athletic Bilbao in Spain, Athletic Club Milan of Italy, and Argentina's River Plate are just a few of the many foreign clubs that have English names.

The Fédération Internationale de Football Association (FIFA) formed in Paris in 1904 by Belgian, French, Dutch, Danish, Spanish, Swedish, and Swiss representatives, now governs the international game. The British nations initially refused to join, and the U.S. Soccer Federation was formed in 1913, the same year that the United States joined FIFA.

SOCCER

goal

PELÉ

The man born as Edson Arantes do Nascimento in Brazil would come to be known as Pelé, one of the greatest athletes to play soccer. Through dedication and hard work, he rose to fame on a global scale when he won Brazil's first World Cup. In 1958, at the age of seventeen, he scored two goals, winning the cup for Brazil for the first time. Later, in 1962 and 1970, Pelé led Brazil to more World Cup victories. He was the first person to play for three World Cup champion teams. Pelé called soccer "the beautiful game," and he lived those words.

Every Olympic Games since 1900 has featured soccer, except for the 1932 event in Los Angeles. Women's soccer first made an appearance at the Atlanta Games of 1996. Currently, men have to be under the age of twenty-three, and women must be over sixteen, in order to play soccer at the Olympics.

The Laws of the Game

Soccer's simplicity is part of its popularity; all the sport requires is a field, a ball, and players. The game is played on a rectangular field, sometimes called a pitch, with a goal at either end. The players on the field try to kick a round ball into the

DID YOU KNOW?

The word soccer is derived from the British phrase "Association Football"—(As) soc(iation football) plus "er." Though the word soccer was coined in Britain, today most British people know the game as football, while soccer is the more familiar term in the United States.

goal

goal to score points. The object of the game is to score more goals than the opposing team.

The official rules of soccer are called the "Laws of the Game" and are reviewed each year at the General Meeting of the International Football Association Board (IFAB). The modifications are included in the publication of a new rulebook each year. According to the Laws of the Game, some of the official rules may be legally altered in matches for players less than sixteen years of age, for female players, for veteran players (over thirty-five years of age), and for players with disabilities. The permissible rule changes include:

- field size
- size, weight, and material of the ball
- size of goals
- game time
- number of substitutions

BASICS

A soccer field must be rectangular and marked with lines to show the boundaries of play. The long sidelines are called touchlines and must measure between 100 yards (90 m) and 130 yards (120 m) long. The end lines, called goal lines, must measure between 50 yards (45 m) and 100 yards (90 m) wide. The painted lines themselves must all be of the same width, and not more than 5 inches (12 cm). International matches have different, more limited field size requirements.

Additional lines are marked on the field to mark the half line, the center circle, the corner arcs, the goal area, and the penalty area. The half line is a

goal

line at midfield marked parallel with the goal lines. The center of the field is marked and a circle with a radius of 10 yards (9.15 m) is drawn around it. Flag posts must be placed at all four corners and each corner is marked with a quarter circle with a radius of 1 yard (about 1 m). The goal area—a rectangle in front of the goal—extends out 6 yards (5.5 m) from each goalpost. The penalty area is a larger rectangle around the goal area that extends 18 yards (16.5 m) along the goal line from each goalpost and 18 yards (16.5 m) into the field. A dot or line is made 12 yards (11 m) out from the middle of the goal line to mark the penalty spot.

There is a wide range of acceptable sizes for a soccer field, or pitch. According to the laws of the game, the field must measure 100–130 yards long by 50–100 yards wide.

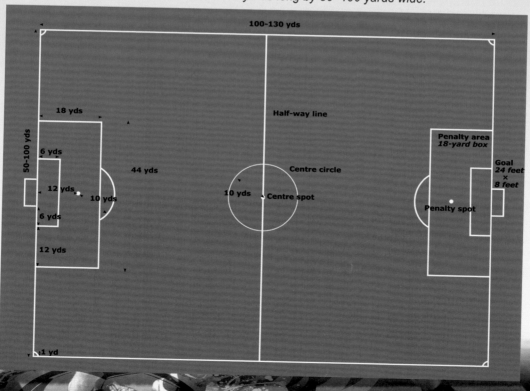

100–130 yds

50–100 yds

18 yds

6 yds

12 yds

10 yds

6 yds

12 yds

44 yds

Half-way line

Centre circle

10 yds Centre spot

Penalty area
18-yard box

Goal
24 feet
x
8 feet

Penalty spot

1 yd

goal

Goals are placed in the center of each goal line. A goal is 8 yards (7.3 m) wide and 8 feet (2.4 m) high. The goalposts may be made of wood, metal, or another material, but must be white and round or **elliptical** in shape so as not to be dangerous for players. Nets are often attached to the goal, but must not interfere or pose any danger to the goalkeeper.

Each team consists of eleven players—ten field players and one goalkeeper. The field players include a defensive line, a midfield line, and an offensive line. The defenders (or fullbacks) help protect the goal, the offenders (or forwards) try to score goals, and the midfielders (or halfbacks) run up and down the field helping with both defense and offense as needed. The only player that can touch the ball with his hands is the goalkeeper; he is only allowed to do this when the ball is in the penalty area. FIFA rules allow only three player substitutions during an official match.

A soccer match lasts ninety minutes with one fifteen-minute break at halftime. When a ball is kicked off of the field, the opposing team gets the ball and throws it in from the sidelines or kicks from a corner. Each match is managed by a referee,

During play, the only players on the field who are allowed to touch the ball with their hands are the goalkeepers. However, if a ball goes out of play over one of the sidelines, it is sent back into play with a throw-in—shown here.

SOCCER

goal

who controls the game, enforces the rules, and can reprimand or eject players who commit fouls.

A foul is any action that is not permitted in the rules, such as striking opponents, physical contact that doesn't deal with the ball, dangerous play, cheat-

When a player commits a foul, such as grabbing another player's shirt, the other team receives a free kick. This is an opportunity to kick the ball from the place of the foul with no interference allowed from the penalized team.

goal

Free kicks can be direct or indirect. A player can shoot the ball directly into the goal and score on a direct kick, but an indirect kick must touch at least two players before a score can result from it.

ing, and cursing. If foul play is committed, the opposing team is granted a free (or place) kick. If the foul takes place in the penalty box, it may result in a penalty, which is a free shot at the goal defended only by the goalkeeper. If a player commits a serious foul, she may receive a yellow card. Two yellow cards, or one very dangerous foul, will result in a red card and ejection from the game. When a team loses a player because of a red card, the team is not allowed to replace that player and must play "down a man."

goal

The World Cup

The World Cup is the biggest soccer event in the world. The first World Cup tournament was held in Montevideo, Uruguay, in 1930. Officials chose Uruguay as the host country for the World Cup because the Uruguay national team had won the gold medal at the Olympics of 1924 and 1928. In the first world cup, the United States beat Belgium and Paraguay but lost to Argentina in the semi-final match. Uruguay won the first World Cup, beating Argentina 4–2.

Brazil has consistently performed well internationally. Brazil has won the world cup on five occasions and some of the most talented and best-known soccer players are from Brazil. Other countries with more than two World Cup championships are Italy (4) and Germany (3).

The world cup is the largest soccer tournament in the world. Every four years, 32 teams from around the world compete to be crowned World Cup champions.

Best results

- Champion
- Finalist
- Semifinals
- Quarterfinals
- 2nd Round
- 1st Round

□ Hosts

Former participants: Czechoslovakia, East Germany, USSR and Yugoslavia (both SFR and FR Yugoslavia shown)

goal

A penalty shot is a special type of free kick that is awarded for fouls committed in the penalty box. This is truly a free shot on goal, with a single player facing off against the keeper. About 85% of penalty shots result in goals.

Today, soccer is truly a global sport. In 2006, thirty-two nations from the Americas, Europe, Asia, and Africa competed against each other in the World Cup, which was hosted by Germany. Billions of soccer fans watched the matches on television and witnessed Italy claim its third World Cup championship, when Italy defeated France in a shootout to win with a final score of 1–1 (5–3 in penalty shots). The 2010 World Cup was hosted by South Africa, the first African nation to be granted the honor of being the host country.

SOCCER

goal

Soccer in America

Though generally not considered a major sport in the United States, soccer has been growing in popularity in America since the 1990s. About 18 million Americans play soccer; 78 percent of these players are under the age of eighteen. There are teams for girls, boys, older children, and young adults. Many adults play in **informal recreational** leagues that are often co-ed. Each state in the country has its own soccer association and the American professional soccer league—Major League Soccer (MLS)—is more than ten years old. The MLS attracts more supporters and some of the top athletes in the country.

The United States has vastly improved its international standing in soccer. The men's national team has appeared in the past five World Cups, and in 2010 was ranked eighteenth in the world and second in the Confederation of North, Central American and Caribbean Association Football (CONCACAF). An increasing number of national team players play in leagues around the world, such as the Premier League in England. The United States women's national team is world-class and has won two of the three women's World Cups and Olympic Gold medals. The women's youth team won the first FIFA Under-19 championship.

Opportunities to Play Soccer

The best thing to do if you are interested in pursuing a professional soccer career is to join a local team as early as possible. Most successful professional soccer players began their careers before or during high school. Soccer can be played anywhere by anyone; find a local team so you can benefit from receiving coaching advice.

DID YOU KNOW?

In the tournament's early years, the term "world cup" wasn't accurate, since only four teams from Europe participated; there were no teams from Africa, Asia, or Australasia.

goal

MIA HAMM

Mia Hamm, born in 1972 as Mariel Margaret Hamm, is one of the most famous female soccer players. Now retired, she played as forward for the United States women's national team, appearing in 275 matches and scoring 158 goals for the team. She was named the women's FIFA World Player of the Year in 2001 and 2002 and was chosen by Pelé as one of the FIFA 125 best living players. Her success and fame has made her a role model to young female athletes.

College sports have also grown. There are now more than 2,500 colleges that play the game; there are more soccer than football teams at the college level. Boston College, Clemson, North Carolina, St. John's, St. Louis, Stanford, U.C.L.A., and Virginia are all colleges with major men's soccer teams. Leading colleges for women's soccer are: the University of Connecticut, Penn State, Pepperdine, Portland, Stanford, Santa Clara, University of Tennessee, Texas A. & M., and U.C.L.A.

Close to 50,000 soccer scholarships are available at campuses across the country. Scholarships usually cover the athlete for four years of schooling and can amount to $100,000 worth of tuition fees, books, and room and board. Academic achievement is a factor for being eligible for a scholarship as well

goal

as being a good athlete. The U.S. Soccer Foundation offers a few select high school students the chance to graduate straight into professional play. There are also many amateur teams in all states looking for players.

Many former players make a career out of coaching at the high school, college level, or even international level. Successful coaching requires a different set of skills than playing on the field. The best coaches develop their skills after many years of training and experience. Youth soccer programs offer a chance for young players to volunteer as coaches and learn whether they might be interested in pursuing a coaching career later in life.

Many soccer players go on to coaching after their playing careers are finished. Young players can also volunteer as coaches for youth soccer programs in their communities.

goal

The head referee runs the game from the field. He is supported by linesmen on the sidelines who help make calls that he can't see clearly.

Refereeing is another career opportunity available to players interested in staying in the soccer world after their playing days have ended. Referees must have extensive knowledge of the laws of the game and must be comfortable enforcing these rules on the field. Players and coaches can become aggressive, and the best "refs" are those who know the rules and are able to hold their ground in the face of conflict. Again, young players can often receive referee training and gain some experience in this career by working for local youth soccer programs.

Soccer, above all, is about fun. You can have the most fun if you are fit and injury-free, whether playing in a World Cup final or just having fun with friends. Take time to develop your skills, improve your fitness, and prepare mentally, and you will discover just how beautiful the game actually is.

SOCCER

2
Mental Preparation & Equipment

Understanding the Words

Proactive *means being prepared in advance.*

To **visualize** *means to picture in your mind, to imagine.*

Tactical *has to do with tactics, the plans and details you come up with as you work to reach a certain goal.*

goal

Staying safe is everyone's responsibility on the soccer field. Parents, coaches, and players need to make sure that safety guidelines are followed closely.

Being safe happens both off the field and on it. Off the field, make sure to get enough rest, be alert, and have a good diet. On the field, players should make sure they are always in control of their movements and are respecting other players. Safety doesn't just happen and isn't just a list of things not to do. Safety consists of being proactive about playing the game responsibly, and well.

Success in soccer depends on four things: commitment, confidence, control, and concentration.

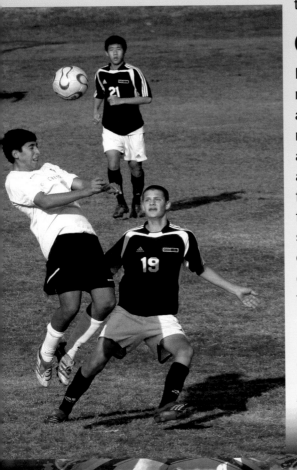

Commitment

If you are committed to a goal, you will need to visualize what you would like to achieve. A possible goal could be to have more endurance or to shoot with more accuracy. Work toward your goal gradually in small steps. Then increase the difficulty of your task, for instance running farther and farther distances or practicing shots from farther away when working on accuracy. Make sure that you practice consistently. The more often you practice, the greater your results will be.

Learning to head the ball is important for all players on the field. Offensive players can use a carefully placed, hard header to score a goal, while defensive players usually head the ball up and away from their goal.

goal

HEADING THE BALL

If a coach tells you to "use your head" in a soccer game, he may not be referring to mental preparation. Heading the ball is the act of striking the ball with the head instead of the foot. When attempting to head the ball, watch it at all times and try to judge where it is going.

- Standard header: Lean your head back, then bring it forward to meet the ball with your forehead. The power of your header depends on how fast you move your head forward.
- Back header: Meet the ball with the rear of the top of your head. Power depends on how quickly you move your head toward the ball.
- Side header: Start with your head somewhere near your shoulder, then bring it up to meet the ball when it is upright.
- Glancing header: Your head should meet the ball and attempt to steer it in another direction.

A lack of height is not a disadvantage if you have the right timing, the ability to hang in the air, and sufficient power. England's Michael Owen, for example, is not particularly tall, but he heads the ball well.

SOCCER

goal

Confidence

One of the best ways to ensure success is to expect it. If you practice consistently and attain more control over the ball, then you'll experience a high boost in self-confidence. A strong attitude is as valuable as skill.

Here are some confidence-boosting thoughts that are especially useful if playing a more experienced or talented team:

- No matter how skilled the other team seems, they are only as good as their next game.
- Your rival team has the same number of players, who are only human, just like you.
- Think that if you play your absolute best, your team can beat the more experienced team.
- Remember, anything can happen—and anything often does happen.
- The only surefire way to lose is to think you will. Never lose the will to win. By keeping confidence, you can take advantage of any situation.

Superstition

Soccer players and coaches have often had many superstitions. Carlos Bilardo, an Argentinean coach, for example was well known for his many beliefs in what would cause his team victory. On their first match against Italy, Bilardo did not have toothpaste so he went to a player's room to borrow some. Because his team won the tournament, Bilardo made a practice of borrowing toothpaste from the same room, same time and same player throughout the entire tournament. Some of his other strange superstitions included carrying a statue of the Virgin Mary to games and banning players from eating chicken (because he believed it brought bad luck). The coach consistently linked

goal

SPORTS PSYCHOLOGY

If you think you'd like to work with athletes and have an interest in psychology, then sports psychology might a career option you want to consider. A master's degree is required for most positions; to teach you would have to go through more schooling to get your Ph.D. There are many programs exclusively for sports psychology, and a few graduate schools do offer specialized degrees. You can also take classes either in clinical psychology or counseling and then specialize in sports later on.

Sports psychologists are increasingly being used in soccer, especially on teams that play at the international level. While coaches are good judges of their player's abilities, sports psychologists can also look into the mental factors that go into each player's performance, including motivation levels and alertness. Sports psychologists aid coaches in forming teams with differing psychological approaches to soccer.

Sports psychologists often use relaxation exercises, mental imagery, and self-hypnosis to help players calm down. During mental imagery sessions, players picture themselves performing skills and actions during a game. Self-hypnosis allows players to focus their attention. Other techniques include goal setting, concentration, and self-confidence sessions.

SOCCER

goal

TACKLING

Tackling means blocking another player who has the ball, then trying to "steal" the ball from that player. You must touch the ball before you touch the player; otherwise it is a foul. Using the bottom of your foot to tackle is also a foul because it could result in serious injury.

- Block tackles: Use your foot to rob a player of the ball by blocking the progress of the ball.
- 50/50 ball: When the ball is equidistant from you and your opponent, you obviously want to get there first. If you can, try to make a short pass to one of your teammates; if not, go for a block tackle.
- Interceptions: Taking control of the ball when it is passed or dribbled.
- Barging: It is legal to lean into a player with your shoulder when he has the ball.

Hitting is not allowed, but you can couple leaning with a sliding tackle. Tackling from behind is dangerous and illegal and will result in a free kick for the opposition and probably a caution for you.

SOCCER

Learning how to tackle and steal the ball from another player effectively is an important soccer skill, but it is difficult. Players perfect complicated footwork and ball-handling skills to avoid having the ball stolen.

victories to seemingly unrelated factors that happened before the game. For a period, Carlos made his players travel via taxi because they won a game after hailing taxis once when their bus broke down.

Game Tactics

A soccer player will be coached in many different defensive and offensive tactics. Playing as a team is crucial to soccer; if the best soccer player in the world were playing with a noncooperative team, he would not go far. A

goal

coach will come into a game with a plan and will instruct his team prior to the game as to what their strategy in the game will be. The coach may want to take advantage of a hole in the rival team's defense or he may have noted a particularly weak offensive player when watching the team's last game.

Soccer players need to understand commonly used terminology. The following is a sample of the **tactical** ideas and terms that a coach will use:

• Pressure: When playing defensively, the defenders should increasingly add more pressure on the ball as it moves to the goal line. A

The two players in blue are "pressuring" the player in between them in an attempt to steal the ball away from him.

goal

Equipment

The Laws of the Game require certain clothing and equipment. Players are not allowed to use equipment or wear jewelry that is dangerous to other players. The basic required equipment includes a jersey or shirt with sleeves, shorts, shin guards, socks (that must cover the shin guards completely), and proper footwear.

defense player can mark the opposing team, which means she does anything to prevent the player to pass or continue toward the net. Applying pressure does not always mean trying to steal the ball, and at times herding, which is moving a player toward a direction she doesn't want to go in order to steal the ball, can be more effective than an all-out attempt to regain possession. If the offensive player is confronted directly, she can easily go around the defensive player. Herding and marking both gradually limit the offensive player's options until she must give up the ball.

- Slowing down the game: When your team is up on points, your coach may want to slow the pace of the game. This does not mean deliberately wasting time; instead your team should attempt to keep possession of the ball for as long as possible while trying to score again. If your team has more points, the more time your team keeps the ball, the less time the other team has to win points back. To keep possession, an effective team will make accurate passes. Also, individual team members must control the ball precisely when they have possession. This combination of good team playing and individual talent helps not only keep the ball but also wins games.

goal

SOCCER SHOES

A soccer shoe should:

- completely cover the foot.
- have a rigid heel.
- have a flexible front to the foot.
- have a wide sole.
- have good padding on heel and sides.
- be made of leather.
- fit snugly on the foot.

OTHER EQUIPMENT

Most players who suffer injuries to the lower leg are not protected by adequate shin guards. The best shin guards have ankle pads that offer both protection and support.

Soccer socks are made from a tight-fitting fabric that enables your pads to be held in place. This fabric holds the pads in a firm grip and allows the feet and legs to breathe and moisture to escape.

Shorts should fit loosely for the sake of mobility. If extra support for the thighs is needed, a player could wear spandex shorts or cycling shorts.

Soccer shorts and shirts are made of lightweight materials and are porous, which allows for sweat to escape and the clothes to stay dry. Some players wear undershirts in cold weather. Any undershirts should be lighter and should not have any seams (to reduce chafing). Female soccer participants should also wear a good sports bra and possibly a supportive sports undershirt.

SOCCER

goal

LOOKING AFTER YOUR SOCCER SHOES

A good soccer shoe is a soccer player's best friend. Make sure that you look after them between games.

- When you take them off, untie the laces properly.
- Remove soil or mud by banging the shoes against a wall, and use a brush to get the rest off. Then wipe the shoes with a damp cloth. Never use soap or detergent to clean your soccer shoes—you will damage the leather.
- If they are wet, stuff them with newspaper (to keep them in shape), and allow them to dry. Do not dry them with a hair dryer, or you could crack them.
- When dry, polish and coat them with a waterproof polish or spray.
- If your shoes have screw-in cleats, grease them occasionally to prevent rusting.
- Damaged cleats can cause serious injury—replace broken ones.
- Never overtighten screw-in cleats—you will damage the threads.
- Avoid walking on hard surfaces, such as concrete or stone, when you are wearing cleats.

SOCCER

GOALKEEPERS

Goalies require specific equipment of their own. Their shoes should preferably have screw-in, long cleats because the mouth of the goal can get very muddy. Shin guards should also be worn.

On hard playing fields, long pants are the best option. These provide padding down the sides of the legs, for cushioning dives. On normal playing fields, shorts should be worn. These, too, have padding, and provide protection.

A goalkeeper's jersey must be a different color from either of the teams playing. Goalie jerseys should also provide padding, especially down the arms and the sides.

Gloves are one of the essential parts of goalkeeping equipment. They are specifically designed for goalies. The gloves you choose should have a rubber covering at the front and should also be well padded with a fastening at the wrist.

In very sunny weather, goalies may want to wear a hat to keep the sun out of their eyes.

goal

Goalkeepers wear special equipment—a padded shirt and shorts to protect their body, and gloves to protect their hands (and to help them make saves with the tips of their fingers).

THE BALL

Soccer balls are made in three sizes, from the small-sized number three to size five, which is used in professional games. While training, learn the ball that suits you best.

Different balls are appropriate for different playing surfaces. On grass, a leather ball with a waterproof coating is most suitable. On a concrete or other hard outdoor surface, choose a plastic one that is regulation weight. Regulation weight, according to FIFA rules, is no more than 16 oz (450 g) and no less than 14 oz (410 g) at the start of a game. For wooden surfaces indoors, there are specially made balls that have a covering similar to tennis balls.

3
Physical Preparation

Understanding the Words

To **transition** *means to change from one activity or state to another.*

Your **hamstrings** *are the tendons and large muscles around the back of the knee.*

Capacity *is how much you can do or perform.*

Warm-Up

An athlete should warm up a half-hour before a match. Cold muscles snap or tear more easily. Warming up means literally exactly that: raising the body temperature by doing light exercise. Start by walking briskly, then transition into a gentle trot, finally sprinting. Try exercises that loosen the joints: shoulder rotations, side bends, torso twists, and knee lifts.

SIDE STRADDLE

By sitting with legs spread, hold one ankle with both hands and move your knees toward your chin. While you do this, keep the leg straight. Hold into this

This soccer team is demonstrating a variety of stretches.

goal

position for five seconds. Repeat this five times and do the same for the other leg. This will help loosen your shoulders and stretch calves and hamstrings.

SEAT STRETCH

Sit with legs together, stretched straight in front of you. Hold each ankle; bring your chin toward the knees. Hold for five seconds and then repeat five times.

QUAD STRETCH

While lying on your back with one leg straight, bend the other leg bent at a 90-degree angle and press your knee to the floor. Hold this position for five seconds, repeating this five times. Alternate with the other leg.

KNEES TO CHEST

Lie on your back, bend your knees, and bring them toward your chest. Hold the position for five seconds, then repeat five times.

FORWARD LUNGE

With one leg bent 90 degrees, stretch your other leg as far as you can, with your foot on the floor. Lean forward and hold for five seconds. Repeat this five times. Reverse the position of your legs and repeat.

THIGH STRETCH

Stand with feet apart. Bend one leg to 90 degrees, keeping the other leg straight. Hold the position for five seconds; repeat five times. Reverse the position of your legs and repeat.

HAMSTRING AND CALF STRETCH

While standing, cross feet. Touch your toes and hold the position for five seconds. Repeat five times. Reverse the position of your feet and repeat.

goal

SOCCER

goal

THE BEST PLAYERS IN THE WORLD

The right combination of natural talent, commitment, and hard work can bring success to a young soccer player. In some cases, these qualities can carry the player all the way to the top. In the months leading up the 2010 World Cup, ESPN ranked the top fifty players of the competition. These players have proven themselves for both club and country and are now considered the best in the world. According to this list, the top ten players are:

1. Lionel Messi of Argentina
2. Cristiano Ronaldo of Portugal
3. Wayne Rooney of England
4. Kaka of Brazil
5. Xavi of Spain
6. Didier Drogba of Ivory Coast
7. Andres Iniesta of Spain
8. Fernando Torres of Spain
9. Steven Gerrard of England
10. Michael Essien of Ghana

Wayne Rooney, who plays for Manchester United and England, is considered one of the best soccer players in the world.

goal

CALF STRETCH

Lean against a wall with hands straight out in front of you and one leg bent to 90 degrees. Stretch the other leg as far as is comfortable while keeping your foot on the floor. Lean forward and hold the position for five seconds, repeating five times. Reverse the position of the legs and repeat.

Training

The importance of training cannot be overstated. No other major sports are played on bigger fields or last as long as soccer. The average soccer player runs between four and seven miles (6–11 km) per match! One study found that in a match, 24 percent of a player's time is spent walking, 36 percent jogging, 20 percent running, 11 percent sprinting, 7 percent walking backward, and only 2 percent of a player's time is spent in possession of the ball. Soccer

LANDON DONOVAN

Good fitness is key to a soccer player's success on the field. Landon Donovan is an American soccer player who plays as forward or attacking midfielder for the United States national team and for the MLS club Los Angeles Galaxy.

Donovan has built a strong soccer career out of his speed, his determination and stamina, and his ability to score goals. His high level of fitness has helped him lead two MLS teams to win championships and has made Donovan the all-time leader in scoring and assists for the United States national team.

goal

Landon Donovan

goal

taxes the body at unmatched levels. A player needs to train her body to deal with the levels of stress that are involved in soccer.

The two major categories of exercise are aerobic exercise and anaerobic exercise. Aerobic exercises consist of getting the heart to beat harder, allowing oxygen to travel through the body more freely. Anaerobic exercise creates muscle mass and does not make the heart or lungs more tired. A soccer player may need different amounts of aerobic exercise depending on his position. A midfielder covers more of the field and so needs to concentrate on aerobics more than offensive players who need to work on quickly reacting muscles.

WEIGHT TRAINING; ANAEROBIC EXERCISE

While soccer is a 90 percent aerobic activity, anaerobic training makes a big difference to the other 10 percent. A player needs strong muscles to forcefully kick the ball. For soccer players, however, the goal of weight training is not to get bulky big muscles in the arms or torso. Ideally, weight training will instead make leg muscles strong and fast with outstanding endurance.

Plyometrics

Plyometric exercises are practiced to increase muscle-response time so that a soccer player can react quickly to new situations on the field. Here's a list of plyometric guidelines:

- Do these activities at the beginning of your training session.
- Even if you're not tired after performing plyometrics, do not continue with other exercises immediately.
- Work out at as fast a speed as possible without losing the quality of what you are doing.

goal

The leg press is a weight training exercise used to strengthen muscles of both the upper and lower legs. Changing the angle of the sled or the position of the feet can change which muscle group is being worked.

- Do not overdo these exercises; two sessions per week with a full day of rest spaced between the workouts is ideal. Also, if you feel soreness or acute pains, then stop doing plyometric exercises.

SOCCER

goal

A full game of soccer involves a lot of running. Jogging during the offseason is a good way to build your aerobic fitness and endurance.

goal

PLYOMETRIC EXERCISE

This exercise is called "Bounding." To train using bounding you must set out small cones and obstacles three feet apart in a straight line. Then, in a semi-squat position jump as far and high as possible over each obstacle. (Anything can be used as an obstacle to be jumped over instead of the cones.)

AEROBIC FITNESS

The more endurance teams have, the better they can perform, especially near the end of ninety-minute games. Soccer players who have the benefit of aerobic training will also be able to recover faster from a tiring sprint. The following are a few suggestions for achieving greater aerobic fitness.

- Long-distance jog: Run at half your **capacity** for two miles or more. If you do this once every three days you will greatly benefit your heart rate, circulation, and lungs.

- Medium-distance run: Run close to your full-potential speed for one mile. This exercise tones leg muscles and also has aerobic benefits.

SOCCER

4
Common Injuries, Treatment, & Recovery

Understanding the Words

A **Stress fracture** is a hairline crack in the bone, especially in the legs or feet, caused by putting repeated strain or pressure on that bone.

Something that is **inflamed** is red, hot, and swollen.

Ligaments are the stretchy bands of tissue that connect bones together at the joints.

Ultrasound treatments use high-energy sound waves to make painful joints and muscles feel better.

Rehabilitation is the process of getting something back to normal.

Contusions are bruises.

Physical therapy treats pain or injury without medication, using exercise and massage.

Your **groin** is the area around where your leg meets your torso.

Something that has been **immobilized** is unable to move.

goal

Medical doctors use the P.R.I.C.E. treatment often for minor injuries:

P: Protect, stop training, and avoid any unnecessary activity.
R: Rest; take the weight off of injured area.
 I: Ice, apply ice pack for around twenty minutes repeating hourly for four hours.
C: Compression, wrap injury with bandage or tape.
E: Elevation, raise the injured part of the body to reduce swelling.

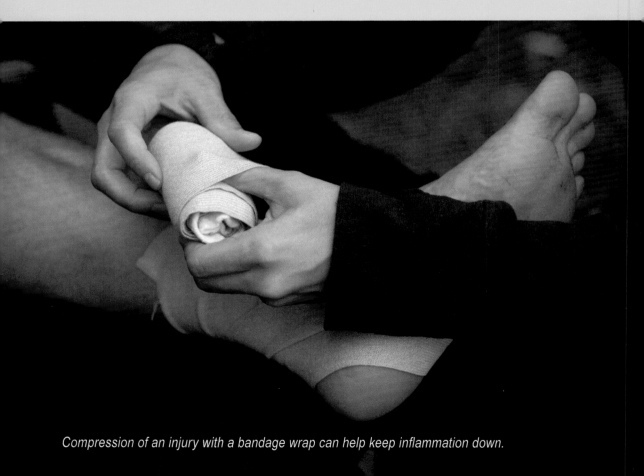

Compression of an injury with a bandage wrap can help keep inflammation down.

goal

OVERUSE INJURIES

An overuse, or chronic, injury, is caused by repeating the same action many times. This is not as serious as an acute injury, but any chronic problem may become worse if not cared for early on, so players should seek medical advice and treatment. Overuse injuries have both mental and physical symptoms:

- unusual tiredness or fatigue
- feeling very emotional, particularly depressed, anxious, or stressed
- a lack of appetite
- an inability to sleep at night
- muscle soreness and cramps
- stiff, painful, or unstable joints
- painful tendons
- pain that shows no improvement for more than three days

Foot

Minor foot injuries can be treated by the PRICE method. A sharp, burning pain in the sole of the foot may point to a cracked metatarsal, which is one of the long bones leading to the toes. This is a **stress fracture**, and the athlete would need to use crutches for a week. Fractures can take from six to twelve weeks to heal.

goal

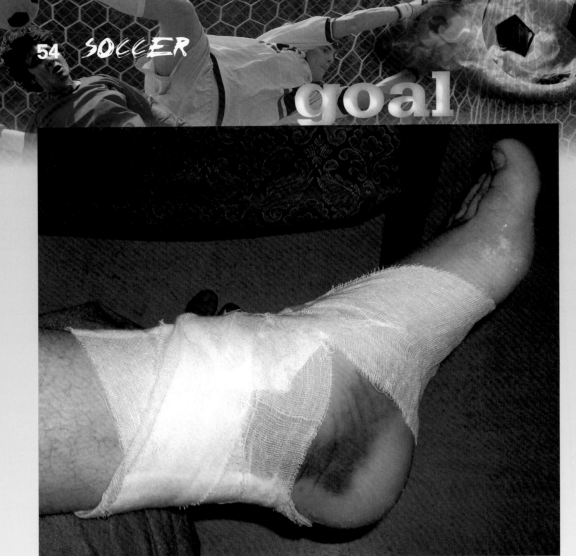

Sprains of the ankle can cause a lot of swelling and bruising. The best treatment is rest, ice, compression, and elevation, or R.I.C.E.

If the base of the heel feels tender, the player could suffer from an **inflamed** tendon. Players suffering from this need to rest their feet and take anti-inflammatory medication. Rolling the damaged foot back and forth over cans of frozen juice a few times daily will reduce pain or swelling.

goal

Ankle

The most common ankle injury is a sprain. The stretching or tearing of ankle ligaments causes a sprain. Symptoms include joint instability, pain, and swelling. An emphasis should be placed on the rest element of the PRICE method; no weight should be placed on the ankle for twenty-four hours or more. Ice should be applied to the swollen ankle. Elevating the ankle will reduce swelling. Massage and physical therapy should be used, as well as anti-inflammatory medication and ultrasound treatments.

A broken or fractured ankle is characterized by sudden, severe pain and bruising. The broken area will be tender and bruised, and there will be great pain if weight is put on it. The injured athlete should elevate her leg and have a shin splint fitted. Broken ankles require medical attention. They can take up to six weeks to fully heal, but it could take months before a soccer player can safely play.

The Achilles tendon connects muscle in the lower leg to the heel bone. If the Achilles tendon is strained it will feel tender and swollen. If the tendon is ruptured, the soccer player will feel the tendon snap and will be unable to raise his heel or point his toes. An athlete with this injury should raise and rest the leg and seek medical attention as soon as possible. Surgery may be required; doctors can treat the injury by putting the leg in a cast. The rupture takes up to ten months to heal, and more time will be needed to get back into shape to play soccer again.

Lower Leg

Shin splints are a type of muscle strain that cause pain in the front of the lower leg. They are caused by overuse or from running on hard surfaces. Shin splint symptoms include pain, swelling, lumps, and redness on the inside of the shin. The injured athlete should use the PRICE method to reduce pain. Heat treatment should be used on the injured area, and the shin should be

goal

taped until swelling stops. Medical treatment is often necessary, and treatments can range from anti-inflammatory medication to massage sessions and physical therapy.

Calf

Strains in the calf result in a sharp pain. The injured player should use the PRICE method and make sure to keep weight off her leg for two days. Anti-inflammatory medication should be used. After the pain and swelling subsides, resume light exercise while being conscious of overextending the body.

Knee

The most common knee injury is known as patella femoral pain syndrome, also known as runner's knee. The second most common is Osgood Schlatter disease, caused by pain and bumps below the kneecap. Use the PRICE method for damages that can heal within a few days. For severe injury (characterized by sharp pain and swelling), seek medical treatment. Extreme cases may require surgery. Ultrasound and physical therapy are both other treatments that may be recommended by a doctor.

Knee ligaments can be damaged, including the medial collateral ligament, which is inside the knee, and the lateral collateral ligament on the outside of the knee. If the ligament is injured, it will feel sore to the touch and painful when the knee is bent. At first, the player should use the PRICE method. The leg should rest from major activity for three to eight weeks. Surgery may be required for serious sprains, followed by three months of rest, and then followed up with **rehabilitation** exercises.

Knee injuries are common in soccer, and surprisingly about 70% of serious knee injuries are non-contact injuries.

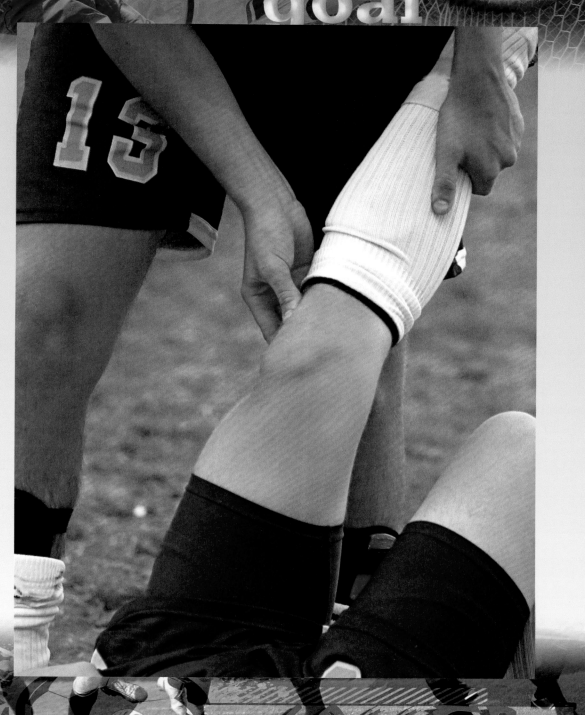

goal

COMING BACK FROM AN INJURY

Clint Dempsey is an American soccer player who plays for both the United States national team and Fulham, an English Premier League club. He is known for his toughness—he once played two games with a broken jaw before his team trainer diagnosed the injury.

In January of 2010, Clint seriously injured his right knee during a game against Blackburn (another club in the English Premier League). At first, it was feared that he had torn his PCL, would need surgery, and would not be available to play for the United States in the World Cup in June. Luckily, a scan of the knee showed only moderate damage. A two-month period of rest and rehabilitation for his knee brought him back to the field and to top form much faster than anyone expected.

goal

Anterior or posterior cruciate ligament (ACL/PCL) injuries are the most severe knee injuries, caused by twists or blows to the knee. Symptoms include instability, swelling, and severe pain, especially when the lower leg is moved. The injured player should use the PRICE method first and ask for medical help. These injuries usually require surgery. Rehabilitation from major knee damage can take up to a year.

Thigh

Contusions known as dead legs are a common injury in a contact sport. They are caused when a muscle is crushed against the bone. Minor contusions

Collisions between players often result in bruises, which can range from minor surface bruises to deep muscle or bone contusions, which are painful and take longer to heal.

SOCCER

goal

vary widely in their severity and can be treated by the PRICE method. Athletes can continue to stretch their quads so long as no pain is caused. Serious contusions involve severe pain and swelling and require immediate medical attention. Doctors can treat major contusions with ultrasounds and surgery. Massage therapy can also help. Recovery time depends on the severity of the contusion, ranging from days to months.

Thigh strains occur when the quadriceps muscles tear. The symptoms are similar to those of contusions. The injured athlete should follow the PRICE method for minor strains, but it can take between three and six weeks before the player is able to fully return to playing soccer. A major tear may require surgery and take up to three months to repair. Ultrasound and massage treatment are used.

Hamstring strains are indicated by pain in that area or the inability to move at all without pain. The pain ranges from minor to serious; the amount of swelling indicates how serious the strain is. The PRICE method should be used for all strains, but severe cases may also require immediate medical attention. Ultrasounds, massages, and **physical therapy** are all used to treat these injuries. Recovery may take a matter of days or could require up to three months. Wearing spandex shorts under soccer shorts may help prevent future thigh injuries.

Groin

Ruptures of abductor muscles due to the muscles stretching too far cause **groin** strains. Treatment for strained groins is the same as strains to the thighs. Minor strain causes slight pain; serious strain can make a person unable to walk. The first thing to do is use the PRICE treatment method. More serious strains require medical help and perhaps even surgery. Lesser injuries can take three to six weeks and if surgery is needed there is a minimum three-month recovery time.

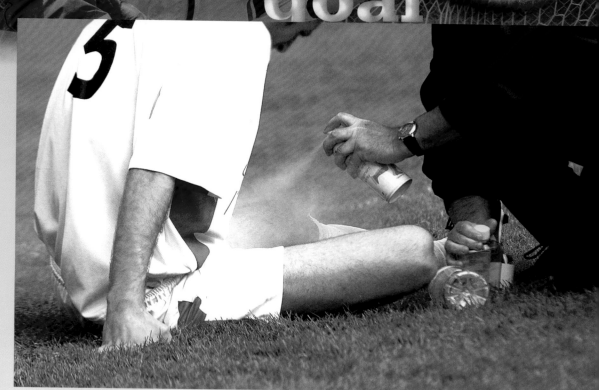

In televised soccer games, it is common to see trainers spraying an injury with something and then sending a miraculously cured player back onto the field. What is this "magic spray?" It is usually a skin refrigerant that freezes and numbs the area on contact and allows a player with a minor injury to keep going.

Hernias are serious groin injuries caused when tissue breaks through the walls of stomach muscles. Lumps in either side of the groin area or stomach appear. Surgery is the only treatment for hernias. An athlete suffering from hernias should seek medical help immediately. Recovery time can take many months.

TYPES OF PAIN

There are many types of pain, and knowing which type you have is helpful when speaking to a coach or doctor. The two major kinds are similar to the classifications of injury: acute and chronic pain. Acute pain is localized, which means that we experience it in one location. Acute pain has been described as a stabbing or piercing feeling, more intense than chronic pain. Chronic pain feels like a gentler, throbbing ache and usually lasts longer than acute pain. If you are injured, try your best to think of ways to describe your pain. Does it feel chronic or acute?

Torso

Abdominal muscle strains are tears in the stomach muscle. The symptoms are similar to thigh and calf strain, including feelings of tightness and pain, as well as bruising in the torso area. The PRICE treatment should be followed. When injured, the athlete should allow herself between two and six weeks of rest.

Stress fractures in the lower back are known as spondyloisthesis. They are characterized by an ache made worse by playing sports. Six weeks of rest is ideal when suffering from a back-stress fracture. After a period of rest, the athlete will need physical therapy to strengthen the back muscles.

By falling on the shoulder or elbow, the athlete may sprain his acromio-clavicular joint, which is in the shoulder. The pain from a sprain varies from minor to complete ruptures of the joint that cause a lump near the neck. The

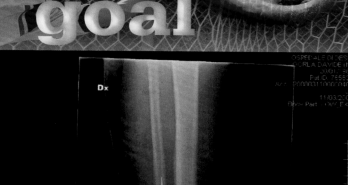

Some very serious bone breaks might need to be set and held together with screws. These X-rays show a lower leg break and how it was set with screws.

PRICE treatment with shoulder exercises can take care of minor sprains, but serious injury requires medical attention, and the shoulder will need to be strapped with bandage or tape. Some shoulder strains can require surgery.

Broken Bones

Any bone breaking is an event that requires medical attention. The injured area should be protected immediately after it happens. Keep the area

goal

SOCCER

goal

immobilized, since any movement could cause the injury to become worse. A brace splint should be fitted as soon as possible. If the skin breaks, producing an open fracture, do not attempt to wash or probe the injured area; cover the ruptured body-part with a clean cloth or tie a bandage. A plaster cast may need to be worn for up to six weeks, but the athlete may need to rest the bone longer before she is able to play soccer again.

Head

A blow to the head, face, or neck can cause a concussion. A concussion has no outward symptoms other than a feeling of fogginess or dizziness. Any player that may have suffered from a concussion should be moved away from play and watched closely. If the situation doesn't improve, medical attention should be sought.

The bruising or swelling of skin on the nose indicates broken noses. Immediate treatment should be used to stop blood flow by plugging the nostrils and applying an ice pack to reduce swelling. If the fracture is serious, the athlete should seek medical attention, especially if the nose is flattened.

Head injuries can occur when two players both jump up to head the ball at the same time.

5
Nutrition and Supplements

Understanding the Words

A **nutritionist** is someone who specializes in helping people eat healthy diets.

Moderation means in the middle—not too much, not too little.

Synthesis has to do with combining two or more substances to create one different substance.

Something that is **fortified** is made stronger than it would have been otherwise.

Controversial has to do with something that people often disagree about.

goal

Playing soccer means more than showing up to practice and games. A soccer player needs to be mindful of what she eats. Doing so will help her be a healthier and safer athlete, a better-functioning student, and a happier person.

Soccer players need to eat a healthy mixture of nutrients to perform at their best. While eating healthy foods is important, an athlete also must decide when to eat, how much to eat, and whether or not dietary supplements are necessary. If you decide to follow a special diet, always consult a nutritionist or doctor.

In general, an athlete needs to eat more than people who are inactive. An active soccer player needs around 2,400 to 3,000 calories to maintain his body weight. All athletes need eat the correct foods to build muscle mass and burn off excess fat.

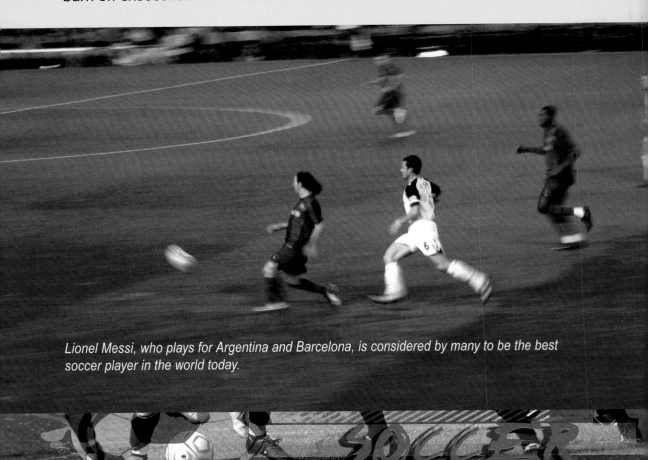

Lionel Messi, who plays for Argentina and Barcelona, is considered by many to be the best soccer player in the world today.

goal

LIONEL MESSI

Lionel Messi is an Argentine soccer player who is widely considered to be one of the best players in the world. Messi showed a natural talent for soccer when he began playing for a local team at the age of five. Diagnosed with a growth hormone deficiency at the age of eleven, Messi was not sure he would be able to attain his dreams until FC Barcelona offered to pay for treatment if he moved to Spain to join their youth league.

At only 5'6 1/2"(1.69 m), he is still a short player, but his height does not affect his playing ability. Being tall is not as important in soccer as it is in some other sports. More important to success on the soccer field are speed, explosive power, agility, skill with the ball, and excellent fitness to allow for all that running. All of these qualities can be aided by the right combination of training and proper nutrition.

When choosing what foods are best to eat, consider the three major food groups: carbohydrates, protein, and fats.

Carbohydrates

Carbohydrates are rich in starch, which is a chemical the body breaks down to get energy. Good carbohydrates include breads, grains, potatoes, cereal, pasta, and rice. Carbohydrates should make up half of your diet. Think of

goal

these foods as the fuel on which your body runs. Some fuel is good for you, however, while others are not so healthy.

Heavily processed carbohydrates, which include sugary foods and white bread, should be avoided. The body breaks those foods down into sugars and then processes them into fat unless they are burned off immediately. Whole-grain foods are best for athletes. Starchy vegetables like potatoes are also very good, since they supply vitamins as well.

Protein

Proteins are important chemicals found in all living things; these chemicals are used to perform specific functions inside our body's cells. Each protein is a long, folded, chain-like molecule made up of "links" called amino acids.

CHOLESTEROL

A lot of bad things have been said about cholesterol—but most of this bad press is focused on LDLs, or low-density lipoproteins, which are a kind of cholesterol that can clog our blood vessels and make our hearts work harder. Our bodies make this cholesterol out of saturated fats, such as those found in animal fat from meats, butter, and whole milk. However, there is a kind of cholesterol known as HDLs, or high-density lipoproteins, which have a good effect on the body. Increasing your HDL levels can be as easy as exercising regularly.

goal

Gender	Age	Activity Level		
		Sedentary	Moderately Active	Active
Child	2–3	1,000	1,000–1,400	1,000–1,400
Female	4–8	1,200	1,400–1,600	1,400–1,800
	9–13	1,600	1,600–2,000	1,800–2,200
	14–18	1,800	2,000	2,400
	19–30	2,000	2,000–2,200	2,400
	31–50	1,800	2,000	2,200
	51+	1,600	1,800	2,000–2,200
Male	4–8	1,400	1,400–1,600	1,600–2,000
	9–13	1,800	1,800–2,200	2,000–2,600
	14–18	2,200	2,400–2,800	2,800–3,200
	19–30	2,400	2,600–2,800	3,000
	31–50	2,200	2,400–2,600	2,800–3,000
	51+	2,000	2,200–2,400	2,400–2,800

Daily caloric requirements depend on your age, sex, and activity level. Athletes, in general, need more calories per day than non-athletes.

Our bodies can break down proteins that are found in foods into their base amino acids and use them to build new proteins that make up our muscles and bones. For this reason, during any exercise regimen, it is important to eat enough protein to give the body the building blocks it needs to become stronger. Eggs, soybeans, rice, and dairy products such as milk and cheese are all good sources of protein. The number of grams of protein you eat should be the same number as one-third of your body weight in pounds. A 200-pound person should eat about 70 grams of protein daily, while a 120-pound person should have about 40 grams of protein.

Fats

Lots of times, we think of fats as bad for us, since eating too much of them is unhealthy. However, fat is an important ingredient needed to make our bodies work correctly. Without fats, our bodies cannot absorb certain vitamins as well. Also, our skin and hair need some amount of fat to grow correctly. However, fats should still be eaten in moderation—no more than 70 grams a day. The best sources of fat are vegetable oils, olive oil, and nuts. Many foods contain saturated fats, which lead to the formation of cholesterol and can force your heart to work harder.

This chart, from the food pyramid at MyPyramid.gov, offers dietary advice for a 2,000-calorie diet. Go to the website to find more personalized and useful information on calorie requirements and healthy diet choices.

GRAINS	VEGETABLES	FRUITS	MILK	MEAT & BEANS
Make half your grains whole	Vary your veggies	Focus on fruits	Get your calcium-rich foods	Go lean with protein
Eat at least 3 oz. of whole-grain cereals, breads, crackers, rice, or pasta every day 1 oz. is about 1 slice of bread, about 1 cup of breakfast cereal, or ½ cup of cooked rice, cereal, or pasta	Eat more dark-green veggies like broccoli, spinach, and other dark leafy greens Eat more orange vegetables like carrots and sweetpotatoes Eat more dry beans and peas like pinto beans, kidney beans, and lentils	Eat a variety of fruit Choose fresh, frozen, canned, or dried fruit Go easy on fruit juices	Go low-fat or fat-free when you choose milk, yogurt, and other milk products If you don't or can't consume milk, choose lactose-free products or other calcium sources such as fortified foods and beverages	Choose low-fat or lean meats and poultry Bake it, broil it, or grill it Vary your protein routine — choose more fish, beans, peas, nuts, and seeds

For a 2,000-calorie diet, you need the amounts below from each food group. To find the amounts that are right for you, go to MyPyramid.gov.

Eat 6 oz. every day	Eat 2½ cups every day	Eat 2 cups every day	Get 3 cups every day; for kids aged 2 to 8, it's 2	Eat 5½ oz. every day

Find your balance between food and physical activity
- Be sure to stay within your daily calorie needs.
- Be physically active for at least 30 minutes most days of the week.
- About 60 minutes a day of physical activity may be needed to prevent weight gain.
- For sustaining weight loss, at least 60 to 90 minutes a day of physical activity may be required.
- Children and teenagers should be physically active for 60 minutes every day, or most days.

Know the limits on fats, sugars, and salt (sodium)
- Make most of your fat sources from fish, nuts, and vegetable oils.
- Limit solid fats like butter, margarine, shortening, and lard, as well as foods that contain these.
- Check the Nutrition Facts label to keep saturated fats, *trans* fats, and sodium low.
- Choose food and beverages low in added sugars. Added sugars contribute calories with few, if any, nutrients.

goal

GOOD FUEL, BAD FUEL

Good Fuel

- low-fat dairy products
- eggs
- fish
- meat and poultry with little or no fat
- cereals and grains
- vegetables
- beans
- potatoes (baked or boiled)
- rice
- legumes
- fruit
- breads (especially whole grain)
- pasta
- water, milk, juice, or sports drinks

Bad Fuel

- any foods with lots of fat—including butter and cream
- burgers, sausages, salami
- potato chips and French fries
- candies and other refined sugars
- chocolate
- soda
- too much caffeine

SOCCER

goal

Dietary Supplements

Many soccer players seek to improve their performance by taking dietary supplements, which are pills or drinks that contain nutrients or chemicals to improve their physical health or performance in the game. Dietary supplements do not include illegal performance-enhancing drugs. Instead, they contain vitamins and minerals, or chemicals that help the body use vitamins more efficiently. Although when used properly, supplements can improve overall health and performance, you should always consult a doctor or some other expert before taking them. Some examples of common supplements include vitamin tablets, creatine, and protein shakes/powder.

VITAMIN AND MINERAL TABLETS

Soccer players need to get certain amounts of vitamins to perform at their best on the field. Ideally, a player should eat foods that are rich in vitamins and minerals, since in general, it is always best to get vitamins and minerals from their original source—food. Sometimes this isn't possible and most American's diets are not as balanced as they need to be. Most of the foods we eat, especially at restaurants, are highly processed and are not as rich in vitamins as they should be. For example, a fish sandwich at a fast-food restaurant will not have nearly as many Omega-3 fatty-acids as a fish bought fresh at a market. This is because most fast-food restaurants fry the helpful nutrients out of foods that are typically nutrient-rich. Not all players have access to unprocessed food, so a vitamin and mineral supplement could be integrated into a healthy diet. These supplements, which are usually taken as a pill, sometimes contain a balanced mixture of vitamins and nutrients (known as a multivitamin), and sometimes they contain a single vitamin or mineral that our diet is lacking.

A mineral or vitamin can be helpful in small amounts but become dangerous in large proportions. You can overdose on vitamins, which can result in a

goal

multitude of side effects that can be strange (your hands turning yellow from too much vitamin A) or downright terrifying (loss of vision, numbness, liver damage). Remember, you can have too much of a good thing! Talk to your doctor before taking any supplement.

CREATINE

Creatine is a protein that's found naturally in the body's muscle cells. When taken in larger doses than usual, it increases protein synthesis in body cells. Athletes who take creatine have more energy to exercise and can improve strength and speed during an exercise routine. Soccer players are often eager to get an extra energy boost from creatine, but this dietary supplement can have negative side effects, such as nausea and vomiting. Some specialists doubt the supplement's usefulness for long-term usage. Always talk to a doctor before taking creatine. And remember, creative is only suitable for adults; if you're under seventeen, you should not take it.

Fat-soluble vitamins—A, D, E, and K—dissolve in fat and can be stored in your body. Water-soluble vitamins—C and the B-complex vitamins—need to dissolve in water before your body can absorb them. Your body can't store water-soluble vitamins, so you need a fresh supply every day.

Vitamin	Sources
A (retinol; carotenes)	milk, eggs; carrots, and spinach
B1 (thiamine)	wheat germ, whole wheat, peas, beans, fish, peanuts, and meats
B2 (riboflavin)	milk cheese, leafy green vegetables, liver, soybeans, yeast,and almonds
B3 (niacin)	beets, beef liver, pork, turkey, chicken, veal, fish, salmon, swordfish, tuna, sunflower seeds, and peanuts
C	citrus fruits: oranges, grapefruits, and lemons
D	produced by human body as a result of sun exposure
E	vegetable oils, nuts, green leafy vegetables, and fortified cereals
K	kale, collard greens, spinach, turnip greens, brussel sprouts, and vegetable oils
Folic Acid	broccoli, peas, asparagus, spinahc, green leafy vegetables, fresh fruit, liver, and yeast
B12	meat, fish, eggs, and milk
B6 (pyridoxine)	cereals, yeast, liver, and fish

goal

PROTEIN SUPPLEMENTS

Getting enough protein from the food you eat can be difficult. Eating protein immediately after a workout is recommended (in order to refuel your body), but most people don't feel up to cooking or preparing themselves a meal immediately after a workout. That's why protein shakes are often a convenient choice. Many shakes contain blends of protein, carbohydrates, and fats, and some include vitamins, to help balance an athlete's diet. Furthermore, having protein immediately after a workout can help repair the damage sustained by your muscles during the workout. However, you should remember that while protein shakes are useful for supplementing your diet, they should not be used to replace normal food in any significant quantities. You can get plenty of nutrients from a balanced diet that cannot be replaced by artificial protein shakes, regardless of how **fortified** they may be. A nutritionist can tell you how to fit protein or supplement shakes into your diet safely and effectively.

GLUTAMINE

Glutamine is a slightly sweet, odorless powder. It aids in the formation of muscles after a workout. It is popular among bodybuilders but it has applications for soccer players as well. Glutamine stops fatigue from intense workouts and raises an athlete's energy level. Research has also shown that glutamine aids in fat loss, and it also has health benefits when used after especially demanding soccer matches. Because of the stress to their bodies, many athletes catch a cold or other illness after major athletic events, but glutamine supplements can help them avoid getting an infection. Glutamine doesn't do much of anything for moderate workouts, however; it only helps for intense workouts.

A few athletes may experience headaches after taking glutamine. Athletes who have kidney disease, liver disease, or Reye's syndrome should not take glutamine, and if a person is sensitive to monosodium glutamate (MSG), she should avoid taking glutamine supplements as well.

goal

CAFFEINE

Caffeine use for athletes is controversial. While some of the information gathered about caffeine use is conflicting, specialists agree that caffeine does not help in high-intensity exercises like a quick sprint. It may, however, help athletes in endurance sports.

So many people (including athletes) drink caffeinated coffee or soda that it is easy to think of caffeine as no big deal. However, caffeine is a stimulant and can have negative side effects that may decrease your game day performance.

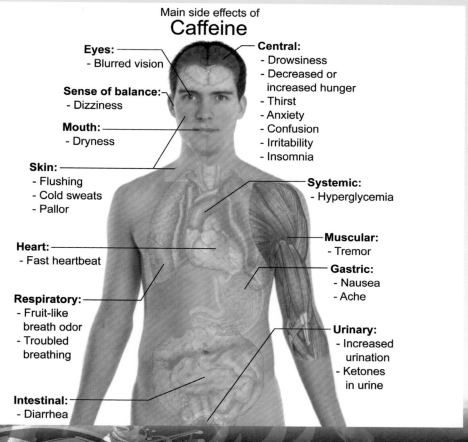

Main side effects of
Caffeine

Eyes:
- Blurred vision

Sense of balance:
- Dizziness

Mouth:
- Dryness

Skin:
- Flushing
- Cold sweats
- Pallor

Heart:
- Fast heartbeat

Respiratory:
- Fruit-like
  breath odor
- Troubled
  breathing

Intestinal:
- Diarrhea

Central:
- Drowsiness
- Decreased or
  increased hunger
- Thirst
- Anxiety
- Confusion
- Irritability
- Insomnia

Systemic:
- Hyperglycemia

Muscular:
- Tremor

Gastric:
- Nausea
- Ache

Urinary:
- Increased
  urination
- Ketones
  in urine

goal

Caffeine motivates the body to use fats as fuel, and caffeine also has mental benefits. Studies have found that athletes feel less fatigued when they have taken caffeine.

If you choose to use caffeine before working out, some sources are better than others. Coffee is not recommended because you never know how much caffeine is in a cup. Other substances in coffee may also get in the way of caffeine's benefits; in a study, treadmill runners' endurance times were

Staying hydrated is essential—soccer players lose a lot of fluids due to perspiration during a game. Water is usually the best choice, but sports beverages are sometimes a good option since they offer some calories and replace minerals lost in sweat.

SOCCER

goal

AVOID SCAMS

Make sure when you buy a dietary supplement that it comes from a reputable source. Ask your physician or pharmacist if a certain product can be trusted. In a study in 2004, scientists found that many products that claim to have creatine actually contain none. Even more alarming was a separate study in 2001, where analysts found out that muscle-gain products contained many chemicals besides the ones that were advertised. Some even included steroids that are harmful to the body and banned from competitive sports.

WATER

Before and after you work out, weigh yourself. If your body lost weight, drink a cup of water for every pound that you lose.

improved when given caffeine, but not when they drank coffee. It is better to drink caffeinated cola and energy drinks because they have a controlled amount of caffeine in them.

Staying Hydrated

A diet is only effective if you are drinking enough water. Dehydration can occur when you don't drink enough water. Symptoms include fatigue, dizziness, and headaches, all of which can hurt your performance in a game or during practice. Carry a bottle of water before a practice or game. Drink water throughout the game to avoid dehydration while sweating.

Staying hydrated has other positive benefits. By drinking enough water in your day you help your mental concentration and improve digestive health.

SOCCER

6
The Dangers of Performance-Enhancing Drugs

Understanding the Words

Something that is **debilitating** *takes energy and weakens a person.*

Narcotics *are a class of drugs that numb the senses.*

Anesthetics *are substances that cause loss of sensation, and some-times loss of consciousness.*

Metabolism *involves all the chemical reactions taking place in a person's body, and has to do with how quickly and efficiently he uses the energy he takes in.*

Stimulants *are substances that cause a person's heart and nervous system to work more quickly.*

Diuretics *are substances that increase urine output.*

Paranoia *is an extreme unfounded distrust and suspicion toward others.*

Infertility *is the inability to have children.*

goal

For many professional players, the pressure to perform well is intense. Athletes face stress from everyone around them to constantly improve their skill, strength, and speed in the game of baseball. The pressure to excel can be extreme for soccer players, and sometimes, an athlete turns to chemical enhancements to reach a level of competitive play that she would not normally be able to achieve.

What Are Drugs?

In general, a drug is anything that you place into your body that changes your body's chemistry in some way. Drugs can be useful or beneficial, such as the tablets you might take when you have a headache or antibiotics developed to fight diseases. Steroids are drugs useful for certain people with **debilitating** conditions that cause their muscles to waste away, and steroids can also be used to decrease inflammation. However, many drugs, including anabolic steroids, can have serious negative effects on your health.

Why Do Athletes Use Them?

Athletes may choose to abuse drugs for various reasons. Here are some of the most common:

- To strengthen muscle: Many athletes want a faster way to build muscle. Steroids and other drugs maximize muscle growth. Simply put, an athlete has to work less hard to gain more when he takes certain performance-enhancing drugs.

- To mask pain: Injuries and strains can cause athletes a lot of pain, and they may be tempted to numb the pain with drugs. **Narcotics** and other **anesthetics** can make an athlete feel the pain less. The high achieved from taking pain-killing narcotics can also be addicting. This

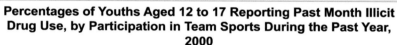

addiction will cause even more problems and, in the long run, even more pain for the athlete.

• Other drugs stimulate the body's **metabolism** and cause athletes to lose weight. Athletes who take **stimulants** or **diuretics** are able to get rid of weight faster. Soccer players, who usually need to be slim to be fast and agile on the field, may find these drugs attractive.

Is Drug Use a Problem for Soccer Players?

For years, officials stated that drug abuse was not a problem for soccer players. In 2007, when growing numbers of bicycling athletes were admitting to

While some young athletes do try to enhance their appearance or performance with illegal drug use, this study from the National Household Survey on Drug Abuse shows that participation in sports actually reduces the drug use among high school students.

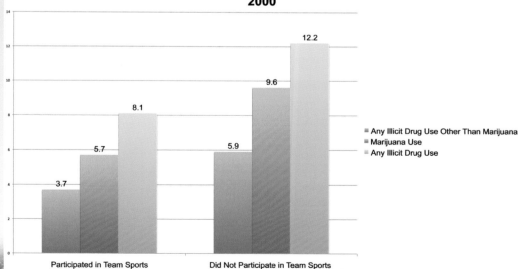

Percentages of Youths Aged 12 to 17 Reporting Past Month Illicit Drug Use, by Participation in Team Sports During the Past Year, 2000

Participated in Team Sports: 3.7, 5.7, 8.1
Did Not Participate in Team Sports: 5.9, 9.6, 12.2

Legend:
■ Any Illicit Drug Use Other Than Marijuana
■ Marijuana Use
■ Any Illicit Drug Use

DIEGO MARADONA

Diego Maradona was one of the world's best soccer players. He helped win the World Cup for Argentina in 1986 and is world-famous for a goal he made in which he maneuvered through six English players and covered 60 meters, becoming what was called "The Goal of the Century." Diego achieved greatness on the field, but he dealt with the problem of drug addiction in his personal life. From the mid-1980s to 2004, Diego was addicted to cocaine. His addiction, of course, got in the way of his soccer playing. After he retired from soccer, his health only got worse. Diego had to be rushed to an emergency room while on vacation in Uruguay. Traces of cocaine were in Diego's blood when he was treated for heart muscle damage. He went to Cuba to follow a drug rehab plan.

Because of his addiction, Maradona would often put on weight and then rapidly lose it. In April of 2004, Maradona went to the hospital for heart problems resulting from a cocaine overdose, and in March of 2007, Maradona went to another hospital in Buenos Aires for alcohol abuse; after he was discharged, he went back after only two days. Diego then went to a psychiatric clinic that specializes in alcohol addiction. In May 2009, he appeared on Argentine television stating that he stopped drinking and had not taken drugs in two and a half years.

goal

drug use, Germany's national football (soccer) coach, Joachim Low, stated, "As far as I am concerned, there is no doping in football [soccer] in Germany."

However, in a BBC study of British soccer players, scientists found that one in twenty of 700-plus soccer players knew a colleague who used performance-enhancing drugs. This shocked many who believed there has not been much drug abuse in soccer. The drugs most commonly abused are stimulants, steroids, and diuretics.

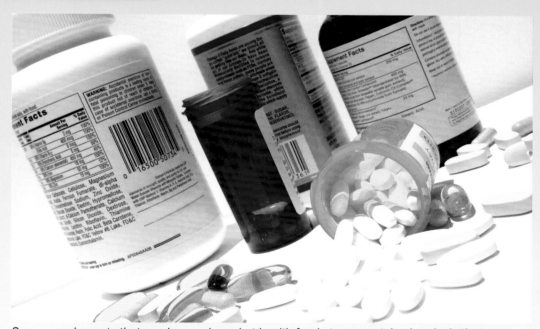

Some supplements that can be purchased at health food stores contain chemicals that are banned and will show up in drug tests, so athletes should educate themselves and read labels very carefully before taking any dietary supplements.

SOCCER

goal

STIMULANTS

Stimulants speed up brain activity and increase alertness. They increase the metabolism, which aids in weight loss. Caffeine is a stimulant. Illegal performance-enhancing stimulants include: Benzedrine, Dexedrine, and Ephedrine. Prescription medications such as Adderall and Ritalin are also considered stimulants, along with illegal street drugs like cocaine.

Stimulant abusers can become addicted. Taking large amounts of stimulants can cause paranoia and feelings of hostility. Also, regularly abusing stimulants can cause dangerously high body temperature and an irregular heartbeat. Heart attack and seizures may sometimes occur.

Besides interfering with the body's recovery time, and affecting athletic performance, alcohol use is illegal for underage athletes. Many high schools have rules that athletes caught drinking will be suspended from the school team.

goal

DRUGS AND SOCCER

David Peplinski had many friends, good grades, and in 2002, was the boys' high school soccer player of the year in Wisconsin. He won a scholarship to Saint Louis University and got a $35,000-a-year soccer scholarship.

And while he did all this, he frequently abused alcohol, marijuana, and prescription painkillers. Eventually, the college kicked him out because of his drug use and drug selling. His life started crashing down. Four men mugged him, stealing his drugs, money, and other possessions. He eventually admitted himself into a hospital for drug-abuse.

Currently, David is drug free and speaks on the dangers of drug abuse. His story is a reminder that in the short term, it is possible to be successful in soccer and academics while on drugs—but in the long run, it is impossible to be an effective athlete and take drugs.

STEROIDS

Steroid use makes muscles cells grow faster from working out. It also affects sex-hormone development. Many athletes abuse steroids to grow muscles at a faster rate than they would if they did not abuse the drug. Steroid use in soccer is not nearly as common as it is in baseball or football, but abuse

goal

GEORGE BEST

One of the greatest players in the history of soccer began his life as a skinny kid from Ireland. George Best grabbed the attention of the English public in the 1960s with his sublime skill, seemingly perfect balance, fearlessness, and incredible self-confidence. When Manchester United won the European Cup in 1968—the greatest prize for a European team—Best was named European Footballer of the Year at the age of twenty-three.

Five years later, Best, a man who could have ruled the soccer world for years to come, gave up world-class soccer and turned his attentions to drinking and other pleasures. The great Pelé described Best as "the best player in the world," while a leading commentator said, "The only tragedy George Best has to confront is that he will never know how good he could have been."

has been reported. In the 2002–2003 season, the Rushden & Diamonds (an English soccer club) goalkeeper Billy Ruley was given a warning for testing positive for anabolic steroids.

Steroid abuse has many negative effects. Hormonal changes include the development of small breasts in males, reduced sexual functions, and **infertility** in males. Anabolic steroid use causes extremely detrimental effects to the heart. While no one should take anabolic steroids without consulting a doctor, athletes especially shouldn't use steroids if they are under the age of eighteen, since teenage steroid abusers are the most vulnerable to severe side effects. Steroids can cause stunted growth and premature sexual development for teens, as well as psychological side effects, including "'roid rage," a surge of irrational anger caused by the chemical.

DIURETICS

Diuretics cause the body to lose water rapidly. They can be used for weight loss and also to attempt to mask drug usage. Side effects include fatigue, tiredness, and vomiting.

Soccer and Alcohol

It is tempting to celebrate a big victory or large achievement by drinking alcohol. You may also be tempted to drink away the pain of defeat. But drinking alcohol can interfere with the body's recovery process and can affect your performance in the next game.

Also, be especially careful to avoid alcohol twenty-four hours after working out if you have any bruises. Alcohol and injuries don't go together, it's best to avoid that after-game drink.

American soccer player Mia Hamm said, "Every single day I wake up and commit to myself to becoming a better player." It is this kind of dedication that will ensure you excel on the soccer field. Prepare yourself mentally and physically, take care of your body, and then simply commit yourself to becoming better and better with each practice and game. Maybe you'll never be Pelé—but you can be the best you can be.

goal

Further Reading

Beasley, Ian and Bob O'Connor. *Soccer Injuries: Their Causes, Prevention and Treatment.* Wiltshire, U.K.: The Crowood Press, Ltd, 2006.

Goldblatt, David. *The Ball is Round: A Global History of Soccer.* New York, N.Y.: Riverhead Books, 2008.

Hunt, Chris. *The Complete Book of Soccer.* Buffalo, N.Y.: Firefly Books, 2008.

Koger, Robert. *101 Great Youth Soccer Drills: Skills and Drills for Better Fundamental Play.* New York, N.Y.: McGraw-Hill, 2005.

LaPrath, Deborah. *Coaching Girls' Soccer Successfully.* Champaign, Ill.: Human Kinetics, 2009.

National Soccer Coaches Association of America. "Soccer Skills & Drills. Champaign, Ill.: Human Kinetics, 2006.

Price, Robert G. *The Ultimate Guide to Weight Training for Soccer.* Cleveland, Ohio: Price World Enterprises, 2005.

Wilson, Jonathan. *Inverting the Pyramid: The History of Football Tactics.* London, U.K.: Orion, 2009.

goal

Find Out More on the Internet

FIFA
www.fifa.com

Major League Soccer
www.mlssoccer.com

Soccer Injuries
www.soccerinjuries.net

SoccerNet
soccernet.espn.go.com/?cc=5901

Soccer Training Info
www.soccer-training-info.com

U.S. Soccer
www.ussoccer.com

U.S. Youth Soccer
www.usyouthsoccer.org

Disclaimer

The websites listed on this page were active at the time of publication. The publisher is not responsible for websites that have changed their address or discontinued operation since the date of publication. The publisher will review and update the websites upon each reprint.

Bibliography

America.gov. "Watching Soccer: a Popular U.S. Pastime," www.america.gov/st/sports-english/2008/July/200807091726180pnativel0.162945.html (25 March 2010).

Business Reference Services. "The Business of Soccer," www.loc.gov/rr/business/BERA/issue3/soccer.html (24 March 2010).

Competitive Advantage. "How Sports Psychology and Mental Toughness Training Can Get You Playing the Best Soccer of Your Life," www.competitivedge.com/sports_article_soccer.htm (25 March 2010).

ESPN. "Clint Dempsey," soccernet.espn.go.com/players/profile?id=39928&cc=5901 (29 March 2010).

ESPN. "Landon Donovan," soccernet.espn.go.com/players/profile?id=19107&cc=5901 (29 March 2010).

Expert Football. "Soccer History," www.expertfootball.com/history (24 March 2010).

FIFA. "2010 World Cup South Africa," www.fifa.com/worldcup (24 March 2010).

International Football Association Board. *The Laws of the Game.* FIFA, 2009–2010.

goal

Lefkowits, John Ph.D., David R. McDuff, M.D., and Corina Riismandel, B.A. "Mental Touchness Training Manual for Soccer," www.cincinnatiunitedsoccer.com/Portals/90/Docs/mentalskills.pdf (25 March 2010).

Sports Illustrated. "America's Obsession with Youth Sports and How It Harms Our Kids," sportsillustrated.cnn.com/2009/more/04/06/youthsports.untilithurts/index.html (25 March 2010).

Sports Injury Clinic. "Common Soccer Injuries," www.sportsinjuryclinic.net/cybertherapist/bysport/football.htm (25 March 2010).

UPMC Sports Medicine. "Soccer," www.upmc.com/Services/sportsmedicine/sports/Pages/soccer.aspx (25 March 2010).

U.S. Youth Soccer. "Coaches Connection Training Activities," www.usyouthsoccer.org/coaches/CoachConnect_LessonPlans.asp (24 March 2010).

SOCCER

Index

goal

Picture Credits

Creative Commons Attribution 2.0 Generic: pg. 15, 32
  acaben: pg. 31
  Art Pets Photography: pg. 48
  Austin Osuide: p. 42
  Ed g2s: pg. 14
  Jason Gulledge: pg 16
  Johnmaxmena: pg. 21
  Linny_heng: pg. 45
  NathanF: pg. 78
  popofatticus: pg. 22
  Sberla: pg. 63
  wjarrettc: pg. 26, 58

Creative Commons Attribution-ShareAlike 3.0 Unported
  Neier: pg. 17
  Sam Ose / Olai Skjaervoy: pg. 54

Fotolia.com
  JJAVA: pg. 85
  Monkey Business: pg. 86
  Tyler Olson: pg. 52

GNU Free Documentation License, Version 1.2
  Adrià García: pg. 68
  Markbarnes: pg. 19
  Roke: pg. 18

United States Air Force
  Master Sgt. Lance Cheung: pg. 37

To the best knowledge of the publisher, all images not specifically credited are in the public domain. If any image has been inadvertently uncredited, please notify Harding House Publishing Service, 220 Front Street, Vestal, New York 13850, so that credit can be given in future printings.

SOCCER

goal

About the Author and the Consultants

J. S. McIntosh is a writer living in upstate New York. He graduated from Binghamton University with a degree in English literature. He enjoys making music on his laptop, playing poker, and being a literacy volunteer. Currently, he writes on topics ranging from military history to health and fitness. For Xandria.

Susan Saliba, Ph.D., is a senior associate athletic trainer and a clinical instructor at the University of Virginia in Charlottesville, Virginia. A certified athletic trainer and licensed physical therapist, Dr. Saliba provides sports medicine care, including prevention, treatment, and rehabilitation for the varsity athletes at the university. Dr. Saliba is a member of the national Athletic Trainers' Association Educational Executive Committee and its Clinical Education Committee.

Eric Small, M.D., a Harvard-trained sports medicine physician, is a nationally recognized expert in the field of sports injuries, nutritional supplements, and weight management programs. He is author of *Kids & Sports* (2002) and is Assistant Clinical professor of pediatrics, Orthopedics, and Rehabilitation Medicine at Mount Sinai School of Medicine in New York. He is also Director of the Sports Medicine Center for Young Athletes at Blythedale Children's Hospital in Valhalla, New York. Dr. Small has served on the American Academy of Pediatrics Committee on Sports Medicine, where he develops national policy regarding children's medical issues and sports.